UNDER THE STREET

BRIAN WARD

ILLUSTRATED BY ANDREW MACDONALD

Kingfisher Books

Educational Advisers: Mary Jane Drummond,
Tutor in Primary Education,
Cambridge Institute of Education, Cambridge
Iris Walkinshaw, Headteacher,
Rushmore Infants School, Hackney, London

The author and publishers are grateful to the
following organisations for their technical advice in
the preparation of this book: Thames Water,
Wessex Water, British Telecom, The Electricity
Council, British Gas, Westminster City Council
and London Underground Ltd.
They would also like to thank the many
individuals who gave valuable help to the
illustrator on site.

Kingfisher Books, Grisewood & Dempsey Ltd
Elsley House, 24–30 Great Titchfield Street,
London W1P 7AD

First published in 1988 by Kingfisher Books

BRITISH CATALOGUING IN PUBLICATION DATA
Ward, Brian
Under the street. – (Stepping stones 4, 5, 6).
1. Great Britain. Underground public utilities
I. Title   II. Macdonald, Andrew   III. Series
363.6
ISBN: 0 86272 361 2

Edited by Vanessa Clarke
Editorial assistant: Camilla Hallinan
Designed by Nick Cannan
Cover designed by Pinpoint Design Company
Phototypeset by Southern Positives and Negatives (SPAN),
Lingfield, Surrey
Colour separations by Newsele Litho Ltd, Milan
Printed in Spain

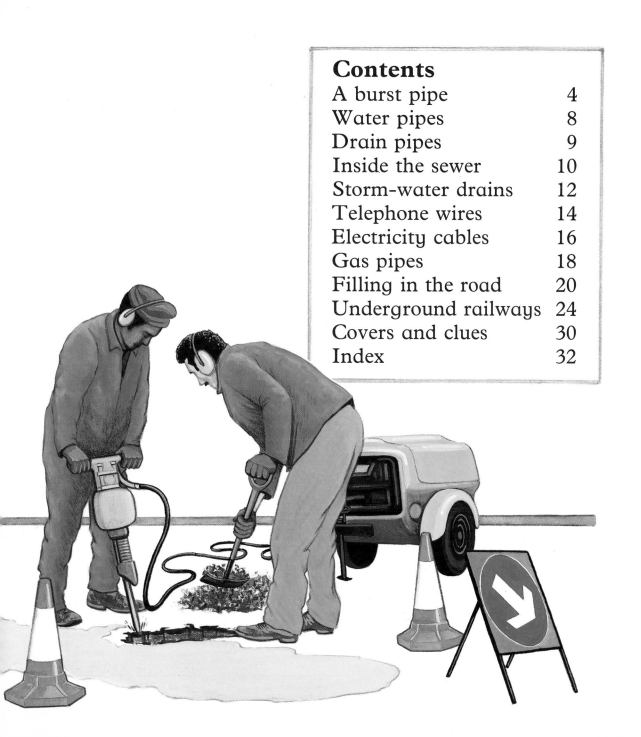

Contents

A burst pipe

Have you ever played games on the covers in the pavement? Interesting things are happening under each one. But we can't usually see what they are unless something goes wrong.

These repair workers have dug a hole to get at a water pipe which has cracked. They turn off the water while they dig and then turn it on for a moment to find out where the leak is. The pipe is a water main.

Main stop-valve cover

The main stop-valve

The pump

A worker shuts off the water in the main pipe by turning the main stop-valve with a long key. The valve is hidden under a metal lid in the road. The workers have brought a pump with them, and it sucks the muddy water out of the hole around the pipe.

The metal collar

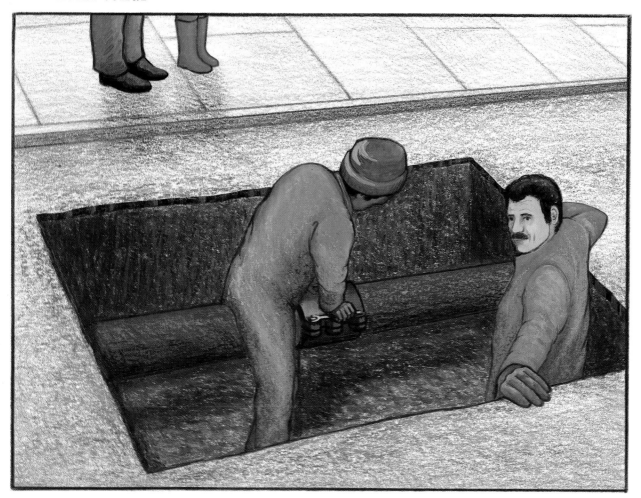

The workers decide that the best way to repair this leak is to fit a metal collar tightly around the crack. They clean off the mud and fix on the metal collar with nuts and bolts. Then they turn on the water again at the stop-valve to make sure that the leak is sealed.

Water pipes

The big water mains bring drinking water into the city from water treatment works and reservoirs.

In every street in the city there are small metal covers in the pavement. They cover the outside stop-valves in the water pipes going from the water main into buildings. Smaller pipes inside the buildings carry the water to taps for drinking, cooking and washing.

Water pipes

Drain pipes

Outside stop-valve cover

Water main

Water pipes

Drain pipes

Outside stop-valve cover

Drain pipes

Whenever you clean your teeth and wash your hands, the dirty water goes down the plughole into drain pipes. Lots more water is used for flushing the toilet and for baths, showers and washing machines. All this dirty water is carried away along the drain pipes into the sewer pipe. The sewer under the street has to be very large because all the dirty water from the buildings in the street pours into it.

Sewer

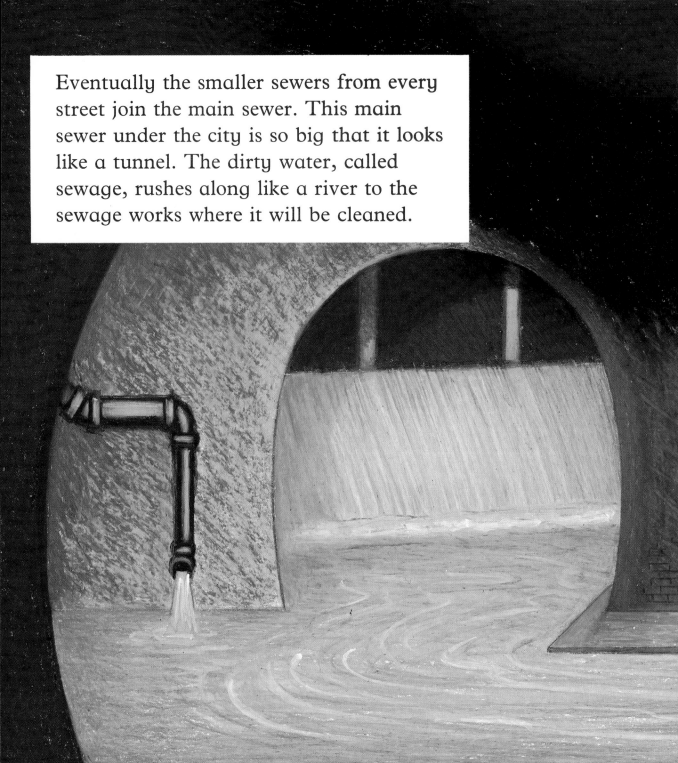

Eventually the smaller sewers from every street join the main sewer. This main sewer under the city is so big that it looks like a tunnel. The dirty water, called sewage, rushes along like a river to the sewage works where it will be cleaned.

Sewage inspectors can get into the sewer through heavy iron plates in the road. The ladder down to the sewer and the paths by the side of the sewer are damp and slippery so the inspectors must take great care. They wear protective clothing too.

Storm-water drains

Up on the street again, rain-water is rushing along the gutter at the side of the road and gurgling down a drain. The storm-water drains carry the rain-water into pipes under the street so that the road is not flooded. Sometimes the pipes carry the rain-water into streams and rivers. Sometimes they carry it to water treatment works inside the city.

Catch-pot

The catch-pot catches leaves and rubbish.

At the treatment works the rain-water is cleaned and made safe to drink. Then the water is pumped through the mains back to the taps in buildings.

Storm-water drain pipes

Treatment works

This rain-water is flowing straight into a stream. The rain-water is still quite clean so it will not pollute the river.

Filter beds

Sand in the filter beds cleans the water.

Catch-pot

Storm-water drain pipes

Telephone wires

Tiny metal wires connect our telephones, and these wires are inside cables under the street. Hundreds of copper wires are wrapped together in paper and plastic to make one thick cable. But the cables are easily

damaged so they are laid inside plastic pipes called trunking to protect them.

Footway box cover

These telephone engineers are replacing a section of cable between two footway boxes. They join the cable wires and make sure that they work by sending an electric signal along each one. They listen for the signal on their earphones.

The telephone engineers reach the cables by lifting lids in the pavement.

Footway box cover

Electricity cables

Deeper down in the earth are the electricity cables that supply power to homes, shops and offices.

An electricity engineer is lifting the cover of a link box to inspect the fuses and cables. Metal wires inside the cable carry the electricity. They make heat so they are covered either with oil-paper or with plastic. Then they are sealed in metal and covered again, sometimes with tarred cloth, sometimes with plastic. The final cover protects the cables from damp and damage by workers digging up the pavement.

Telephone footway box

Electro Hi-Fi

97

Electricity
link box

17

Gas at home

Pushing through new pipes

Gas pipes

Gas comes into our homes along pipes under the ground. Old gas pipes were made of cast-iron and steel and look like water pipes but most new pipes are made of bright yellow plastic which is very strong and long-lasting.

Gas mains carry gas along the road and smaller pipes take the gas from the main to each home.

18

The Mole

Digging a trench

Workers lay the pipes in different ways. Sometimes they can push a new pipe inside an old one. Sometimes they can use a tunnelling machine called a Mole to burrow a tunnel under the ground. Then they push a pipe through behind it. At other times, workers need to dig a trench in the road and lay the pipe inside. After all the pipes have been connected, the engineers test them to make sure that there are no leaks. Then they let the gas through.

Filling in the road

After new pipes are laid and repairs are finished, the workers have to fill in the holes and make the road safe to drive on.

First they pack sand around pipes to protect them. Then they shovel in earth and crushed rock called hardcore, and ram it down with a compactor. Another worker heaps hot black asphalt on top. Finally a roller flattens the surface.

Now the road is smooth enough and strong enough to take the weight of cars, buses and lorries again.

Hold on, Brian. I'm still tamping down this lot.

Compactor

▲ Water main

Gas main

Foundations   Subway

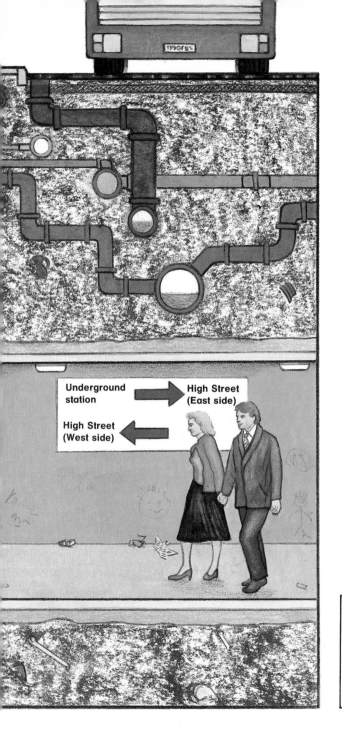

In a busy city, the space under the street is a useful place to tuck away all the pipes and cables. They are out of the way down there and we can't see them but they are busy supplying us with all the things we need every day.

Business people also make use of the space under the street for offices, storage space and car parks. Strong foundations go deep below the surface to support the weight of these buildings.

Tunnels called subways go under the street so that people can avoid the traffic on the busy road and cross in safety.

Can you see?	
A storm-water drain	A water pipe
A sewer	An electricity cable
A gas pipe	A telephone cable

Underground railways

Even further down under the street are the underground railways which carry people quickly around the city. Stairs and escalators go down from the ticket hall to the platforms where trains stop for passengers.

Trains travel on different lines under the city and each line has its own tunnels going from station to station under the ground.

Ticket hall

Escalator

Pathway

Escalator

Stairs

Escalator

Platform

Platform

Train tunnel

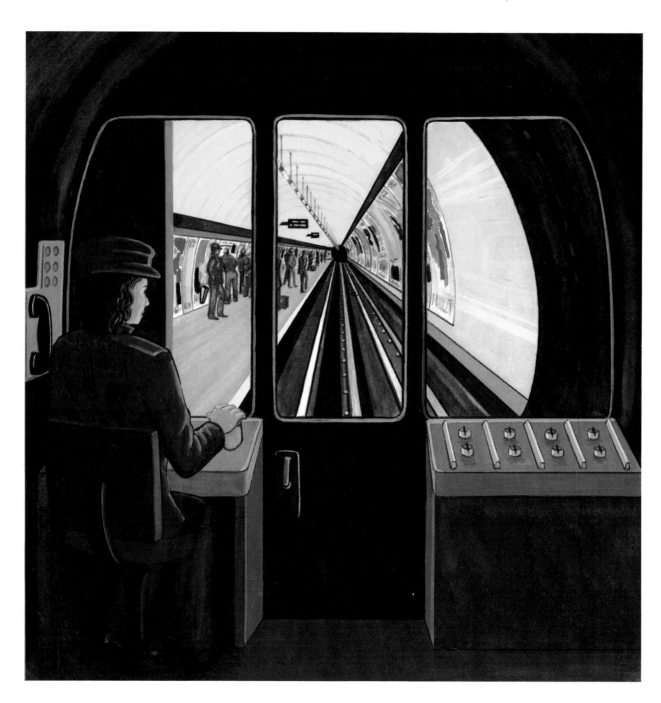

All the tunnels in the station and under the street are round because a round shape is stronger than a square and a rectangular one. The round tunnels are lined with sheets of metal.

Engine car

Driver

Passenger car

Automatic doors

Motor

The shoe which picks up electricity

Wheels

The underground trains look different to ordinary ones because they are shaped to fit the tunnels. The train is powered by a motor which picks up electricity from an electrified rail in the track. The driver controls the train, and watches for the signals telling her when to stop and start the train.

Many people work on the underground railways below the street.

Here are some of the people you see when you go on a train.

Stand clear of the doors, please!

Platform guard

Train driver

Can I see your ticket please?

Ticket inspector

Passengers

You don't usually see these people but they also work on the underground railway.

Controller

Cleaner

Maintenance engineers

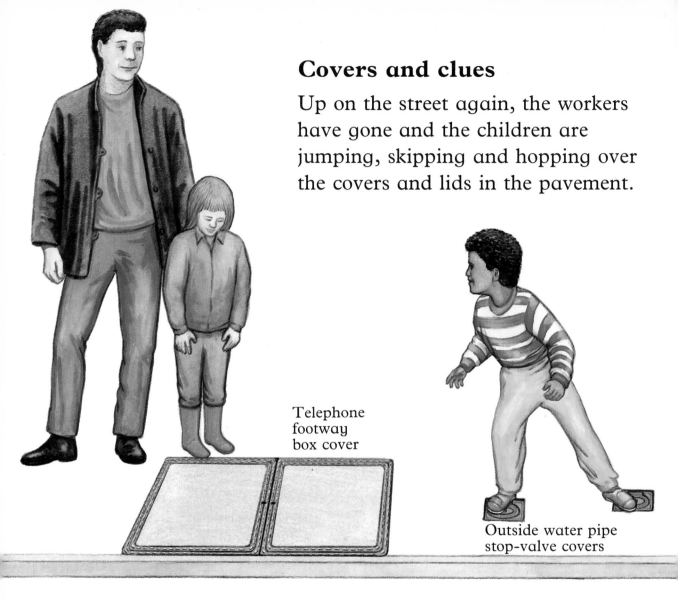

Covers and clues

Up on the street again, the workers have gone and the children are jumping, skipping and hopping over the covers and lids in the pavement.

Telephone footway box cover

Outside water pipe stop-valve covers

Sewer inspection cover

Maybe you have played on them too. Some covers are made of metal; some are made of concrete; and some are made of plastic. Each type is a clue to the busy world hidden under the street.

Telephone footway box cover

Gas valve box cover

Gas valve box cover

Electricity link box cover

Storm-water drain

Water main inspection cover

Index